ATTACK SUBMARINE

Editorial: Steve Parker
Design: David West
                  Children's Book Design
Illustrator: Simon Bishop
Picture research: Cecilia Weston-Baker
Consultant: Captain Andrew Buchanan (Southampton)

Created and designed by
N. W. Books Ltd
70 Old Compton Street
London W1

First published in
Great Britain in 1989 by
Franklin Watts
12a Golden Square
London W1

ISBN 0 86313 970 1

Printed in Belgium

Contents

Hunter-Killer   4
Built for Stealth   6
Hull Design   8
Flying Under Water   10
Power Without Air   12
Navigating   14
Communication   16
Detecting the Prey   18
Weapons   20
Life Under Water   22
Launch to Refit   24
Specialized Killers   26
The Young Engineer   28
Around the World   30
Glossary   31
Index   32

ATTACK SUBMARINE

IAN GRAHAM

GLOUCESTER PRESS

London · New York · Toronto · Sydney

4

The first submarine

Dutchman Cornelius Drebbel is thought to have built the first submarine. He sailed it along London's River Thames in 1620. In 1776, when the USA and Britain were at war, American David Bushnell built the tiny *Turtle*. But it failed to blow up British ships.

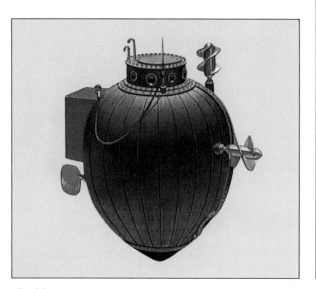

Subs for jobs

There are several different types of submarine, each designed for a particular job. They are classified according to their power source and the weapons they carry. Nuclear-powered attack submarines like *Trafalgar* are known as SSNs. The largest and most powerful nuclear submarines are known as SSBNs. Diesel-powered submarines are coded SS (page 31).

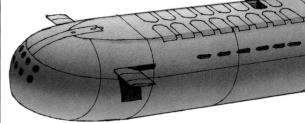

Rudder

The submarine is steered to the left or right by movable panels called rudders. The larger vertical tower towards the front is the fin.

HMS Trafalgar is the first of the British *Trafalgar* class (the group or type) of submarines to be built. Launched in 1981, it entered service with the Royal Navy in **1983. *Trafalgar* weighs 4,500 tonnes, measures over 85 metres long, 10 metres in diameter and can reach speeds of 30 knots (55 kph) when submerged.**

Aft escape hatch

Manoeuvring room

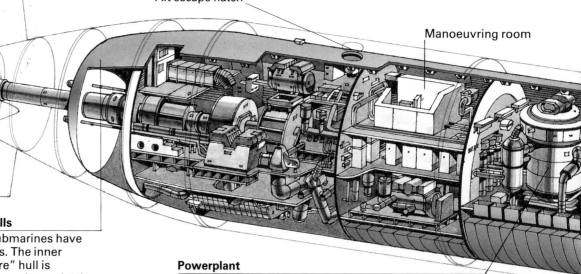

Twin hulls

Many submarines have two hulls. The inner "pressure" hull is strengthened to resist the immense force of the water around the submarine when it dives. The outer hull is streamlined to slip easily through the water.

Powerplant

SSNs like *Trafalgar* are powered by nuclear energy. Heat produced by a nuclear reactor converts water into steam. This drives a turbine which spins a shaft connected to the submarine's propeller, pushing the submarine through the water. The steam also drives generators which provide the submarine's electrical power.

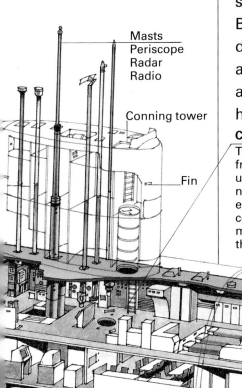

Maritalia (Midget attack)

Los Angeles (SSN)

Typhoon (SSBN)

The modern submarine is a powerful war machine. It can roam the world's oceans submerged and unseen, making it difficult to find and destroy. It can stay at sea for months on end, rarely returning to its base.

Large missile-carrying submarines can strike with enormous force, without warning, and from almost anywhere in the seven-tenths of our planet covered by sea. They are intended to discourage any country from starting another World War. Smaller torpedo-carrying submarines are also deadly, capable of sneaking up and sinking ships of various kinds. Indeed, submarines of all types are such a serious military threat that, in the event of war, it is vital to locate and destroy them. This is the job of the "hunter-killer" – the attack submarine.

The basic engineering problems of building a submarine have been well known for many years. But tomorrow's breed of attack submarine stretches designers and engineers to the limit. It must be fast, quiet and well-armed. It must be able to avoid detection, locate and destroy the enemy, survive attacks and resist the harsh conditions at sea.

Control room
The submarine is operated from the control room underneath the fin. The nuclear powerplant and electricity generators are controlled from a manoeuvring room behind the nuclear reactor.

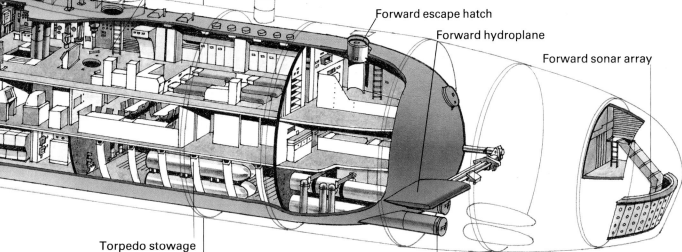

Masts
Periscope
Radar
Radio

Conning tower

Fin

Forward escape hatch

Forward hydroplane

Forward sonar array

Torpedo stowage

Torpedo tubes

BUILT FOR STEALTH

To be effective, submarines must stay secret. The ability to move around undetected is called "stealth" . It is very important in modern warfare. Detection methods are always improving and the submarine engineer must find new ways of defeating them.

Noise is a great problem. Sounds made by a submarine and its machinery can be picked up by the enemy's sonar (page 18) and so give it away. Engineers try to prevent this by making submarines as quiet as possible. The hull is given a smooth, rounded shape that creates very little water disturbance, or turbulence. Turbulence not only makes a noise, it also slows down a submarine, so minimizing it is doubly important. The propeller is another main source of noise. Larger, slower propellers make less sound, while the number and shape of the blades is also important.

Even machinery and crew noise inside the submarine can be detected by other craft. This is reduced in two ways. Machinery is isolated from the hull by mounting it on flexible pads, and the hull is covered by sound-absorbing materials to stop the sound escaping.

Trafalgar was built by the British company Vickers Shipbuilding and Engineering. The hull was made first but one end was left open. Then all the internal equipment was assembled on platforms and slid into the opening. The end of the hull was closed and sealed and the submarine made ready for its launch.

MODULAR BUILDING

Modern submarines are built in giant construction halls divided into several areas. Each area builds a different part or module of the submarine, such as the nuclear reactor compartment or the bow (front) section. When each part is ready, it is moved into the central construction area, where the submarine takes shape. From here, the finished craft is rolled out on wheeled platforms called bogies, or it may be lifted out by a crane.

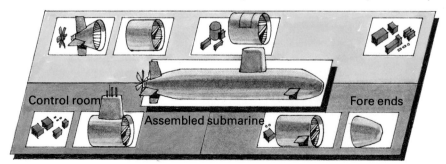

Aft ends   Reactor compartment   Auxiliary machinery

Control room   Fore ends

Assembled submarine

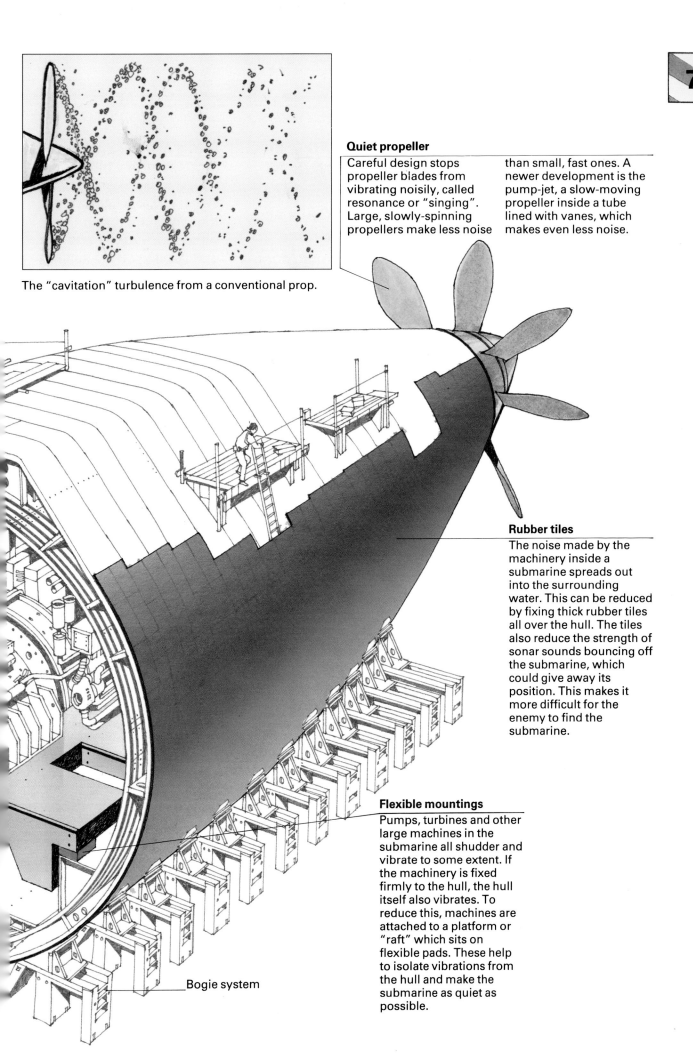

The "cavitation" turbulence from a conventional prop.

Quiet propeller

Careful design stops propeller blades from vibrating noisily, called resonance or "singing". Large, slowly-spinning propellers make less noise than small, fast ones. A newer development is the pump-jet, a slow-moving propeller inside a tube lined with vanes, which makes even less noise.

Rubber tiles

The noise made by the machinery inside a submarine spreads out into the surrounding water. This can be reduced by fixing thick rubber tiles all over the hull. The tiles also reduce the strength of sonar sounds bouncing off the submarine, which could give away its position. This makes it more difficult for the enemy to find the submarine.

Flexible mountings

Pumps, turbines and other large machines in the submarine all shudder and vibrate to some extent. If the machinery is fixed firmly to the hull, the hull itself also vibrates. To reduce this, machines are attached to a platform or "raft" which sits on flexible pads. These help to isolate vibrations from the hull and make the submarine as quiet as possible.

Bogie system

HULL DESIGN

The basic streamlined "teardrop" shape is used by most submarines today. But the hunter-killer's hull must be strong enough to withstand enormous water pressure during deep dives, and also to survive anti-submarine weapons. The engineer can solve these problems in several ways. Submarines may have a single hull, double hulls or multiple hulls. In the double-hull design, the space between the two hulls cushions the inner "pressure" hull from the blast of a weapon. Most Soviet submarines probably have double hulls. In fact the largest Soviet *Typhoon* class SSBNs have two pressure hulls, lying side by side inside a single outer hull.

Trafalgar's pressure hull is covered by an outer casing, but there is a much smaller space between the two than in a true double-hull design. Although it is not so resistant to anti-submarine weapons, this design has other advantages. It is smaller than a double or multiple hull, and so causes less turbulence as it powers through the water. A smaller submarine is also more difficult to find and attack successfully than a large one.

Diving and surfacing

Air trapped in a submarine's ballast tanks makes it float. When water is flooded into the tanks, this makes the submarine heavier and it sinks, or dives. To surface again, air is blown into the tanks.

Surfaced

Diving

Air released through vent valves
Water floods in

Surfacing again

High-pressure air fills tanks
Water forced out

BALLAST TANKS

The space between a submarine's hulls is not empty or air-filled. It is taken up by a series of tanks for storing oil and water. In the double-hull design, the main ballast tanks are also in this space. In a single-hulled submarine, the main ballast tanks are inside the front and rear "cones" – the rounded ends of the submarine.

- Main ballast tank
- Trim tank
- Compensation tank
- Lubricating tank
- Reserve feed
- Battery tank
- Brine tank
- Fresh water tank
- Hydraulic tank
- Bilge tank

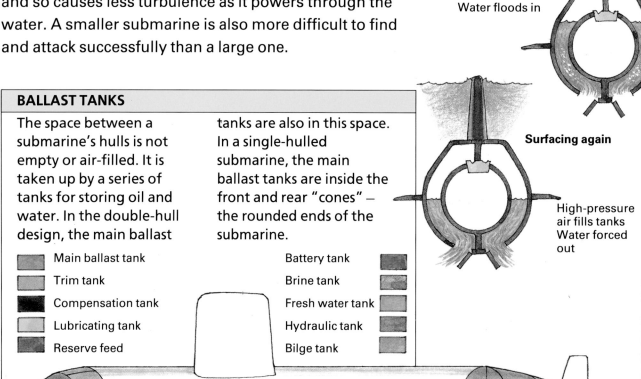

Submarines do not dive as deep as many people think. The average depth of the seabed outside shallow coastal waters is roughly 3,500 metres, and the deepest parts are more than 10,000 metres down. Yet most submarines can only dive to about 300-450 metres. Soviet *Alfa* attack submarines are probably the record-holders. They are thought to dive to 700 metres.

The sea foams as this submarine opens its vents to dive.

The outer hull

The outer hull, the "skin" of a submarine, totally encloses the inner pressure hull and its oil and water tanks. It is built from a metal frame covered by specially shaped metal plates of steel, aluminium or titanium. It has a streamlined "hydrodynamic" shape for travelling smoothly through water.

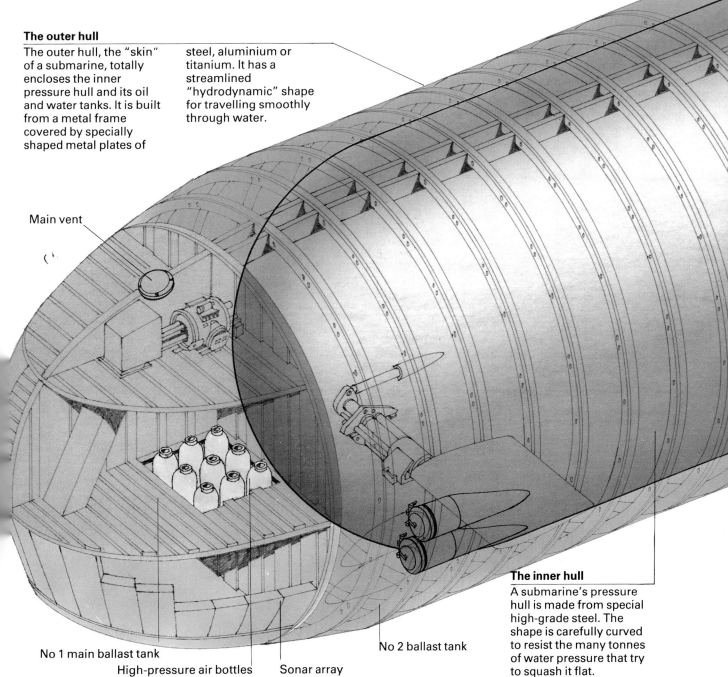

Main vent

The inner hull

A submarine's pressure hull is made from special high-grade steel. The shape is carefully curved to resist the many tonnes of water pressure that try to squash it flat.

No 1 main ballast tank

High-pressure air bottles

Sonar array

No 2 ballast tank

FLYING UNDER WATER

A ship manoeuvres on the sea's surface in two dimensions. A single rudder does the job. But a submarine has to move in all three dimensions, including up and down. Engineers must design controls that enable the submarine's position and depth to be precisely controlled.

In this sense, the submarine engineers are faced with the same problem that airship engineers faced many years ago. The answers are much the same. A submarine is "flown" through water, like an airship is flown through the air. The submarine's rudders and rear hydroplanes are very similar to an airship's rudders and elevators. They work by tilting a large panel, called a control surface, into the stream of water (or air) flowing past. The water presses against the panel and forces it, and the craft attached, to tilt in the opposite direction. It is the simple scientific principle of "action and reaction".

At high speed, a submarine's bow (front) could be pushed round by the water resistance. To solve this, there are an additional pair of control surfaces, the forward hydroplanes, which keep the bow stable.

When a submarine is at "periscope depth", just a few metres down, any slight loss of control could mean that part of it breaks the surface and comes into view. This is one of the many reasons why a submarine must have precise controls.

Diving

The forward hydroplanes are tilted upwards, forcing the bow down. The rear hydroplanes tilt in the opposite direction, raising the stern or "tail".

SHAPING UP FOR SPEED

Until the 1950s, submarines had long, thin hulls. But when submerged, they could be difficult to control at high speed. So US Navy engineers (below) developed a hull shape similar to an airship or a killer whale. This was more controllable at all speeds.

The *Albacore* hull, named after the first submarine to have it, was used by the US *Skipjack* and *Barbel* class attack submarines.

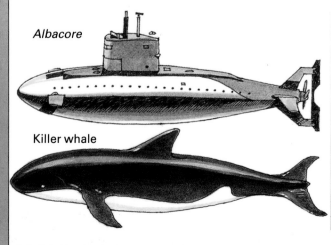

Albacore

Killer whale

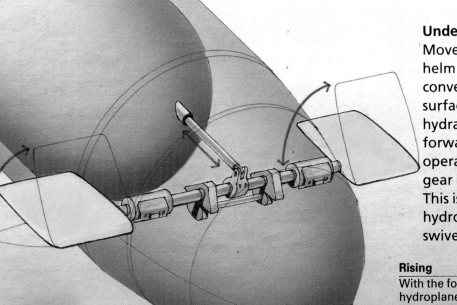

Underwater wings

Movements at the submarine's helm ("steering wheel") are conveyed to the control surfaces by mechanical and hydraulic linkages. When the forward hydroplane control is operated, it makes the tilting gear in the bow rotate a shaft. This is linked to the hydroplanes, which then swivel up or down.

Rising

With the forward hydroplanes tilted down and the rear ones tilted up, the bow rises and the tail sinks – and the submarine rises.

Turning right

If the upper and lower rudders are swivelled to the right, the submarine's tail is pushed to the left. The craft begins to turn to its right.

Turning left

Swivelling the rudders out to the left results in the submarine's tail being forced to the right. The submarine then steers round to the left.

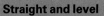

Straight and level

When the submarine reaches the desired depth, its hydroplanes and rudders are set to their mid positions for a straight, level course.

Naval vessels are usually steered by helmsmen, named after an ancient word meaning "rudder". Submarine helmsmen are called planesmen because they control hydroplanes as well as rudders. Instrument panels in front of the planesmen show the submarine's depth, its heading (direction) and its state of trim (its angle in the water).

POWER WITHOUT AIR

Until the 1950s, all submarines used diesel-electric propulsion. Many still do. While they are on the surface, diesel engines provide the power. Diesels need a supply of oxygen (from the air) and produce poisonous fumes. So when the submarine submerges, it must switch to electric motors powered by batteries. The batteries have to be recharged at regular intervals by the diesel engines. This can only be done when the submarine is on the surface, or just beneath with a "snorkel" sticking up into the air above.

During the 1950s, engineers developed a new powerplant that would free submarines from these frequent visits to the surface. As a result, in 1955 the American *Nautilus* became the first nuclear-powered submarine. A nuclear power generator, called a nuclear reactor, does not need an air supply. So nuclear-powered submarines can stay submerged for several months at a time. Some can travel 500,000 kilometres before the nuclear fuel has to be replaced. A diesel-electric submarine needs to refuel perhaps every 15,000 kilometres.

Propeller shaft
Power is transmitted from the steam turbines to the propeller along the propeller shaft. A "clutch" mechanism in the shaft allows the turbines to be disconnected from the propeller when the electric motors take over.

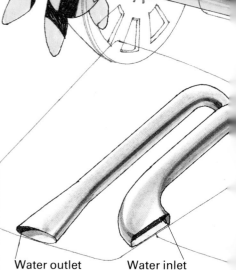

THE PUMP-JET

Trafalgar itself is driven by a propeller (above), but newer submarines in this class use a "pump-jet propulsor" (right). This works by spinning a bladed rotor inside a "shroud" or duct lined with vanes, like a propeller inside a pipe with ridges on the inside. The rotor's speed is much lower than a propeller's, making it much quieter, but without loss of power. The pump-jet is still a fairly secret design (see photograph on the right).

Water outlet   Water inlet

Water pumped through *Trafalgar's* nuclear reactor is used to make steam. The high-pressure steam jet turns the many-bladed rotors of steam turbines, which are connected to the propeller shaft through a gearbox.

Reactor pressure vessel

The reactor pressure vessel contains the nuclear fuel and the "primary" water circuit. This is sealed because, as the water is heated by the reactor, it becomes radioactive. The primary circuit is used to heat a "secondary" water circuit, which does not become radioactive.

Main turbines

The main turbines are the key in converting heat from the reactor into mechanical power. Steam flows through the turbines past the rotor blades. The pressure of the steam against the blades pushes them round and so spins the turbine shaft. This turns very quickly, so the rotations are slowed down by a gearbox before driving the propeller itself.

Turbo generators

Not all the turbines drive the submarine's propeller. One set drives generators, called turbo generators, which produce the submarine's electrical power.

Gearbox

Main motor

Manoeuvring room

Condensers

After steam has passed through the main turbines, a series of condensers converts it back to water, to be used again. Sea water taken in through the rear hydroplanes cools the condensers. As steam flows through the condensers and changes to water, the steam generator uses heat from the reactor to turn it back to steam again.

Diesel generator

If the nuclear reactor should fail or have to be shut down, the submarine has back-up power. *Trafalgar* is equipped with an electric motor powered by batteries, which are charged by a small diesel generator.

Reactor compartment

The nuclear reactor compartment houses the reactor pressure vessel. The reactor must be shielded by thick lead walls to protect the crew from its radioactivity. The reactor is controlled from the manoeuvring room behind this compartment.

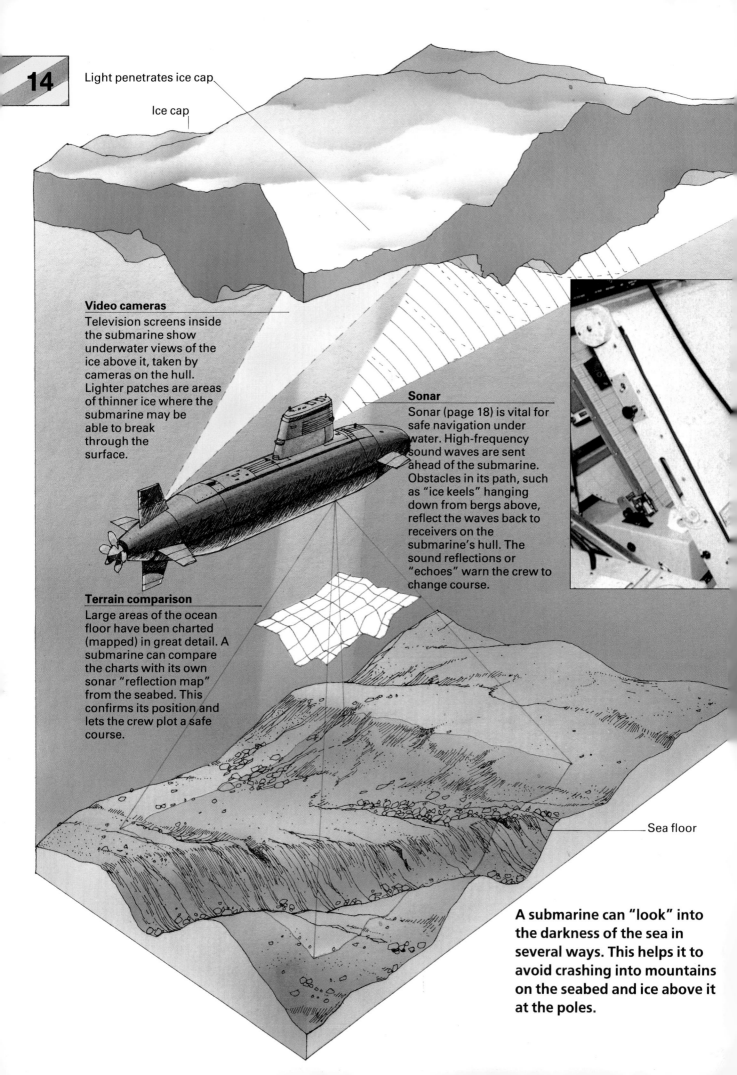

Light penetrates ice cap

Ice cap

Video cameras
Television screens inside
the submarine show
underwater views of the
ice above it, taken by
cameras on the hull.
Lighter patches are areas
of thinner ice where the
submarine may be
able to break
through the
surface.

Sonar
Sonar (page 18) is vital for
safe navigation under
water. High-frequency
sound waves are sent
ahead of the submarine.
Obstacles in its path, such
as "ice keels" hanging
down from bergs above,
reflect the waves back to
receivers on the
submarine's hull. The
sound reflections or
"echoes" warn the crew to
change course.

Terrain comparison
Large areas of the ocean
floor have been charted
(mapped) in great detail. A
submarine can compare
the charts with its own
sonar "reflection map"
from the seabed. This
confirms its position and
lets the crew plot a safe
course.

Sea floor

**A submarine can "look" into
the darkness of the sea in
several ways. This helps it to
avoid crashing into mountains
on the seabed and ice above it
at the poles.**

NAVIGATING

The navigation room
Instruments in the navigation room show the submarine's position. The officers who monitor them may also record position and course on printed charts.

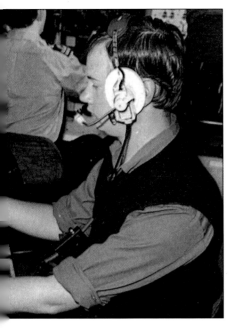

On the surface, a submarine can use the same methods as a ship to determine its position. Radar bounces radio waves off coastlines and other objects, and displays the echoes on a screen. Sightings of landmarks, stars, the Moon and the Sun also enable navigators to "fix" their position. But underwater, these methods are useless.

Engineers came up with a simple answer, in theory. If a submarine's speed and direction are recorded, then its present position can be worked out from its last position. In practice, though, there were difficulties. The effects of tides and currents had to be taken into account, and records of speeds and changes in direction must be extremely accurate. But the problems were solved, and all nuclear submarines are now fitted with the Ship Inertial Navigation System (SINS). It can translate the submarine's movements into a "positional fix" , as latitude (degrees north or south of the Equator) and longitude (east or west). SINS must first be programmed with an accurately-known start point. Then it constantly updates the submarine's position.

SHIP INERTIAL NAVIGATION SYSTEM (SINS)

SINS uses the fact that when a craft accelerates, objects inside it react by trying to stay still (inertia). For example, when a car accelerates forwards, everyone inside it is pushed backwards into their seats. In a submarine, these forces affect the rotation of three gyroscopes spinning at right angles to each other. Forces on the gyroscopes are measured by accelerometers. Electrical signals from the accelerometers are fed into a computer and fix the submarine's position on a map.

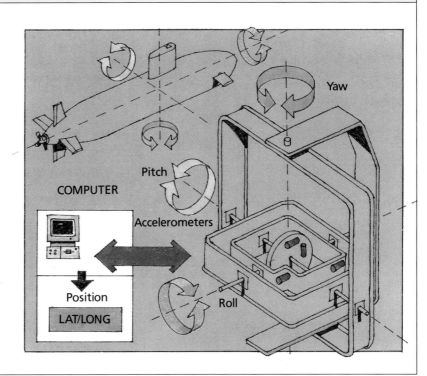

COMMUNICATION

All submarines need to communicate with their bases and other craft. Communicating with a submarine on the surface in peacetime is easy, but "talking" to a submerged submarine in wartime is much more difficult. The high- frequency radio signals normally used in air do not travel in water. Another problem is to get signals into and out of the submerged submarine quickly, reliably and with the minimum risk of detection by enemy forces.

Communications engineers have solved the problem in several ways. The submarine can be brought close to the

A submarine's vertical fin may house up to ten different masts and periscopes of various types.

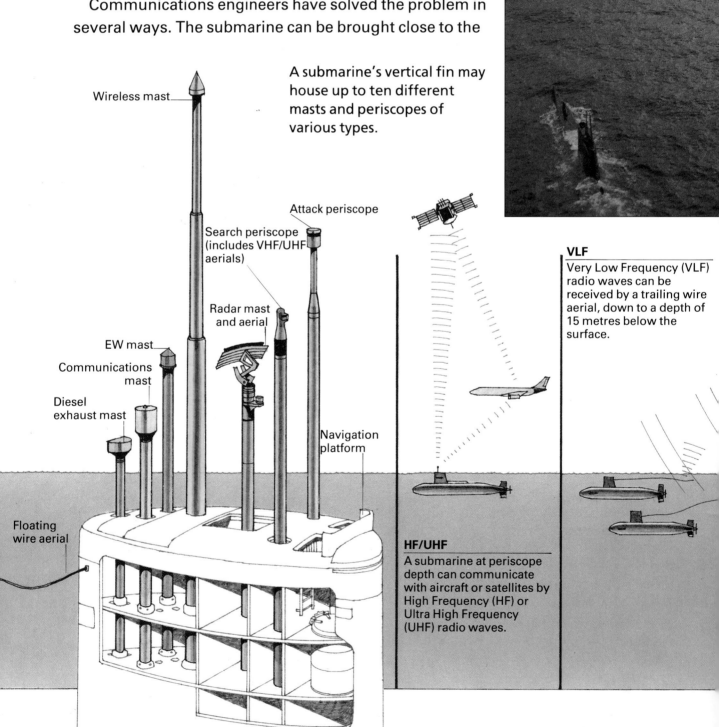

Wireless mast

Attack periscope

Search periscope (includes VHF/UHF aerials)

Radar mast and aerial

EW mast

Communications mast

Diesel exhaust mast

Navigation platform

Floating wire aerial

VLF

Very Low Frequency (VLF) radio waves can be received by a trailing wire aerial, down to a depth of 15 metres below the surface.

HF/UHF

A submarine at periscope depth can communicate with aircraft or satellites by High Frequency (HF) or Ultra High Frequency (UHF) radio waves.

surface so that a radio mast may be extended into the air above. Or the submarine can stay deep and release a long wire aerial or a floating communications buoy. Although high-frequency radio signals cannot penetrate water, lower-frequency signals can. But aerials that transmit such low frequencies are enormous, up to 20 kilometres across! So submarines can only receive at these low frequencies. The low frequencies have another disadvantage. The lower they are, the lower the speed at which information can be sent. So, overall, higher frequencies are preferable.

A military plane flies over a just-surfaced submarine for a brief communications exchange. The sub will soon disappear again below the surface, after arranging its next "rendezvous".

Many different methods of communications are available to the submarine's crew. They use floating radio buoys, trailing wire aerials or direct radio links with aircraft and satellites.

TACAMO

TAke Charge And Move On (TACAMO) uses trailing wire aerials up to 10 kilometres long.

XSTAT

The submarine releases a buoy, which floats to the surface and communicates with aircraft by radio.

ELF

Extremely Low Frequency radio waves pass through water down to a depth of at least 100 metres. They are received by a wire aerial over 300 metres long trailing behind the submarine.

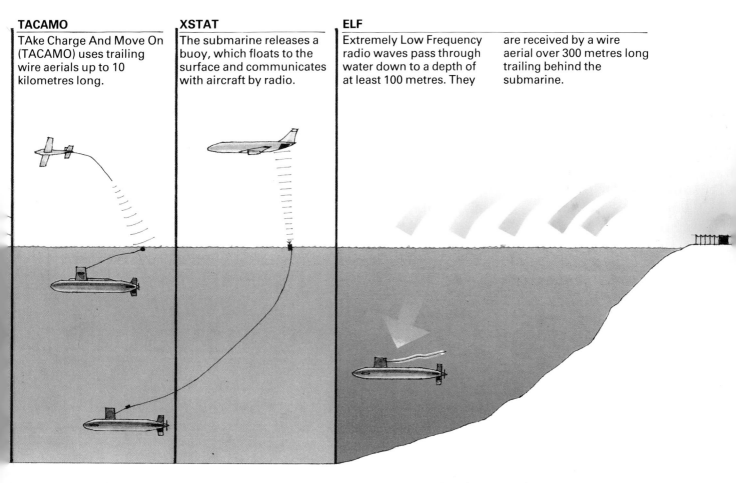

DETECTING THE PREY

The prey of the nuclear attack submarine is nearly always another submarine. But how does a hunter-killer like *Trafalgar* find the enemy, yet remain undetected itself? Sonar (SOund NAvigation and Ranging) is the most important technique. Engineers use the fact that water is a very good conductor of sound. Any noises made by a submarine can be picked up far away by underwater microphones called hydrophones. So fit a submarine with hydrophones on its hull, and it can detect other submarines and ships.

However, it is a two-part problem – for the attack submarine must avoid sonar detection itself. So it is designed to be as quiet as possible (see page 7). For example, nuclear submarines need to circulate water constantly to cool the reactor. But the pumps that do this create noises, which pass out through the hull and can be picked up by sonar. So modern nuclear submarines only use their circulation pumps at speed. Engineers have used the principle that hot water rises and is replaced by cold water for pump-less circulation at slow speed.

Multi-displays
Information from the sonar system is put through a computer and displayed on a screen for the sonar operators. The most modern sonars can show an object's rough size and shape, its position and course, and speed and depth – all on a single multi-coloured television display.

SONAR: "SEEING" WITH SOUND

In active sonar, pulses of sound are transmitted by the submarine, reflected by objects within sonar range, and their echoes are detected by hydrophones. However, active sonar gives away the attack submarine's presence and position to anyone "listening in". To minimize this risk, submarines tend to use passive sonar. The hunter's hydrophones listen for noises from other craft, such as propellers, pumps and other machinery sounds.

Active sonar

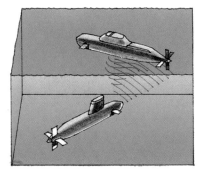

Passive sonar

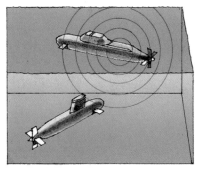

Friend or foe?
Sonar and other information about a vessel is analyzed by computer, to find out if the "contact" is a friend or possible enemy.

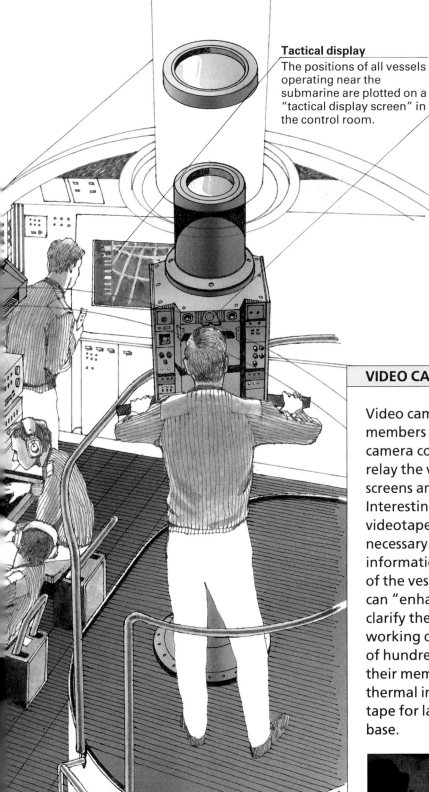

Tactical display

The positions of all vessels operating near the submarine are plotted on a "tactical display screen" in the control room.

Up periscope!

There are normally two periscopes, to look at the surface without the submarine having to appear. There is a general-purpose periscope and a smaller attack one. The modern periscope is not a simple tube with mirrors, but a complex electronic device. Its laser range-finder measures how far away an object is. A dim, dark scene is made clearer by image intensifiers. A thermal imager can produce a "heat picture" of the surrounding sea, even in total darkness.

VIDEO CAMERAS

Video cameras enable several crew members to see the same scene. A video camera connected to the periscope can relay the view at the surface to monitor screens anywhere in the submarine. Interesting images can be recorded on videotape and replayed, in slow motion if necessary. The monitors also show information such as the range and speed of the vessel they are tracking. Computers can "enhance" a confused scene and clarify the shape of another vessel, working on the shapes and silhouettes of hundreds of other craft they hold in their memory banks. The pictures from thermal imagers can also be recorded on tape for later analysis, perhaps back at base.

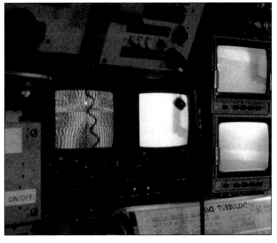

In the control room, the sub crew use advanced electronics, computers and visual displays to search for their prey, monitor friendly and enemy vessels, and avoid detection themselves.

WEAPONS

An attack submarine's weapons not only destroy their targets, but also protect the submarine itself against attack. If a hunter-killer is detected, it may find that it has become the hunted one. An anti-submarine force can include other submarines, surface ships, helicopters and aircraft. *Trafalgar* has five standard torpedo tubes, each 53 centimetres in diameter. To save on space and machinery, engineers have designed various weapons so that they can all be launched through these tubes. The weapons include Tigerfish torpedoes, Sub-Harpoon missiles, and Stonefish and Sea Urchin mines.

Torpedoes are no longer just streamlined bombs with a propeller at the back. To make them more accurate, the engineers have equipped modern torpedoes such as the Tigerfish with their own "on-board" sonar and computer systems. Torpedoes can be used to attack other submarines or surface ships. Sub-Harpoon is an anti-ship missile. It can carry an explosive warhead, weighing 230 kilograms, through the air to a target over 100 kilometres away – at almost the speed of sound.

An attack submarine's main weapons are torpedoes and missiles. Torpedoes stay underwater, while missiles break the surface and fly to their targets.

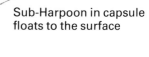

Sub-Harpoon in capsule floats to the surface

Torpedoes, missiles and mines must be "threaded" down through the main hatches and then stored on racks in the torpedo room.

Booster fires

The Sub-Harpoon

A Sub-Harpoon missile is launched inside a capsule from a standard torpedo tube. It floats up and when it reaches the surface, the capsule opens. The missile's booster rocket fires and blasts it out of the capsule. Then the booster drops away and a turbojet engine powers the missile along at low level, homing in on its target ship.

Sub-Harpoon launched from capsule

The Tigerfish

When the Mark 24 Tigerfish torpedo is launched, it is guided from the submarine along a connecting wire. As it nears the target, the wire is released and the torpedo's own sonar system takes over.

Homing electronics

Forward battery

Guidance control

Motor

Warhead

The Stonefish

The Stonefish mine is "laid" from a torpedo tube. It is designed to sit on the seabed, waiting for an enemy vessel.

Guidance wire

TACTICS OF THE HUNTER-KILLER

In wartime, one of the attack submarine's jobs is to keep open important sea lanes for friendly ships. Its sensors and weapons are designed mainly to find and attack enemy submarines and surface ships – it cannot attack aircraft. "Smart" mines such as the Stonefish remain on the seabed and explode only when they detect an enemy vessel nearby. Subroc flies to near an enemy submarine, then dives onto its target.

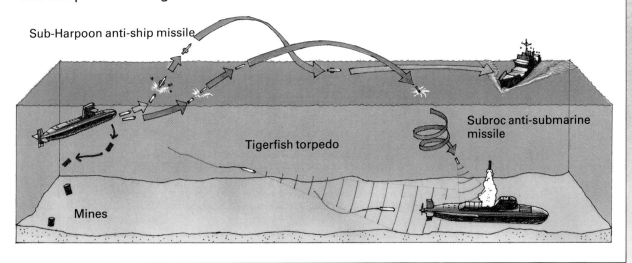

Sub-Harpoon anti-ship missile

Subroc anti-submarine missile

Tigerfish torpedo

Mines

LIFE UNDER WATER

Navigation and weapons present the submarine designers and engineers with great challenges. Another challenge, perhaps less obvious, is how to keep the crew comfortable and working effectively. Comfort is a problem. Make a submarine more spacious and roomy, and it becomes larger and more easily detected. One way of keeping a submarine small without affecting crew comfort is to reduce the number in the crew, by using more automatic systems and machinery. A modern attack submarine such as *Trafalgar* has a crew of about 98, compared to the USA's *Skipjack* of 30 years ago, which had a larger crew of 114 – yet it was smaller in size.

Everything the crew members need must be carried in the submarine. This means necessities such as food, and also entertainment and leisure facilities when off-duty, such as movies and a cinema in which to watch them. There must be a bunk and locker, at least, for every member. The designers must "pack in" cold stores for keeping food fresh, galleys (kitchens) for preparing it, and a mess (eating area) separate from the working areas.

Space is forever limited in a submarine, and the crew always have to put up with cramped quarters such as bunks (opposite). Each member must be assessed psychologically to make sure he can cope with this way of life. All the essentials are here, from medical care (below left) to meals in the mess (below right).

UNDERSEA ESCAPE

The US Navy has two Deep Submergence Rescue Vehicles (DSRVs). Each can dive to 1,500 metres deep and is big enough to take 24 people. The vehicle itself has a crew of four. To help it find the damaged submarine and then "dock" (join) with it safely, the DSRV has a range of complex sonar systems. It manoeuvres close to the submarine using water jets, and powerful lights and television cameras show views of the stricken submarine.

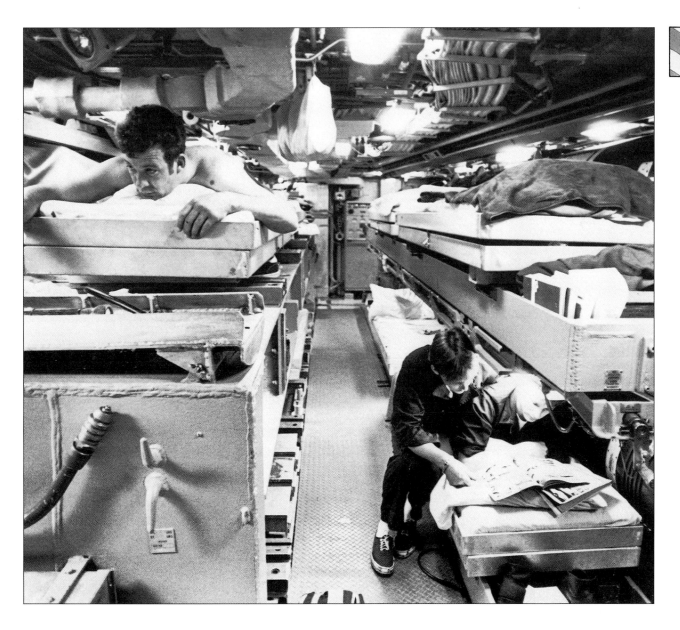

LAUNCH TO REFIT

When a submarine is launched and first touches the water, the engineer's work is far from completed. A year or more of checks, tests and trials is needed before the submarine can be handed over to the navy that ordered it. After handover, a crew is assigned to the submarine. If it is a new type, or contains new equipment, the crew must be trained to use the submarine correctly.

From then on, the submarine's life is a constant series of military exercises and patrols. The crew are kept highly trained and ready for action, and the typical working day is filled with practices, drills and testing of equipment. From time to time the submarine returns to its home base for routine maintenance, taking on stores, and of course for shore leave – the crew's "holiday" .

While the submarine is at sea, the research engineers on shore are busy developing new and better equipment. After some years the submarine may have a refit, a lengthy process when the new equipment is fitted. Finally, a submarine becomes too old for "active service". It may be scrapped, or converted to a target for weapons practice – by the next generation of attack submarines.

FITTING A NEW REACTOR

A nuclear submarine's fuel has to be replaced after several years. Newer reactor cores such as the "Core Z" used by *Trafalgar* last longer than older types. The submarine must return to its base for refuelling. Its reactor pressure vessel is opened, the core with spent fuel is taken out, and a new core is fitted in its place. This procedure must take place under strict safety precautions, to prevent radiation leakage. After testing, the submarine returns to sea for more tests before going back on patrol.

The launch crane

The traditional slipway is now being replaced as a way of launching submarines, by the vertical ship-lift or a "launch crane" (below). The traditional way of launching a submarine (or any other type of ship) is to slide it down a gently-sloping ramp called a slipway. Cradles protect the hull from scraping.

TRIALS PROFILE

Trials begin with the submarine tied up alongside the dock. Its nuclear reactor and electronic systems are powered up for the first time since the launch. It then goes for a "fast cruise", but still tied to the dock, to test how the engine performs at speed. The next stage of the trials involves a test dive, again while still in the dock. Finally, the submarine heads out into the ocean for sea trials, which last about one to two months. During the sea trials the submarine's speed and manoeuvrability are checked to make sure it performs as the engineers expected. Weapons are test-fired, and noise levels are monitored. It then returns to base before the first spell of active service.

SPECIALIZED KILLERS

Some hunter-killer submarines are designed to carry out specialized jobs. In World War II, midget submarines were successful in attacking ships tied up in harbours. These tiny craft are becoming popular again. They have the advantage of being very small and quiet, and so difficult to detect. Some midget submarines are smaller versions of the "full-sized" hunter-killer, with a pressurized hull and able to operate completely on their own. Others are so small, and with such a short range, that they must be used together with a larger "mother-craft", either a surface ship or another submarine.

The Italian *Maritalia* midget is only 10 metres long. It can use a diesel engine for propulsion under water for long periods, which is impossible with a normal diesel-electric engine. Even smaller craft, called "chariots", are so tiny that a crew cannot work inside them. Instead, one or two divers wear breathing equipment and ride on top of the craft. The *Piranha* class of submarines, designed by the British company Vickers for transporting navy divers, carries two of these chariots.

If a full-size submarine cannot approach its target without being detected, it may be possible to use a smaller, quieter craft instead. The midget submarine is taken to within range of the target by a mother-craft, before being released into the water to operate under its own power.

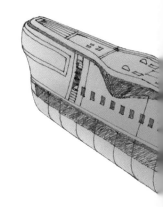

MIDGET SUBMARINES

The *Maritalia* midget submarine is propelled by an "anaerobic" diesel engine. Oxygen needed for burning the diesel fuel is stored inside the "toroidal" (coiled-pipe) hull. Exhaust gases are also stored in the submarine, since pumping them into the sea would allow detection by an enemy. This submarine can travel under water for great distances using its diesel-powered electric motor, which a normal diesel craft cannot do.

Maritalia midget

Periscope

Sonar

Stores

Galley and mess

Pilot console

Oxygen stored in toroidal hull

Diesel generator

Electric motor

Small and secret

The *Piranha* submarines are small diesel-electric craft designed for secret missions using combat divers. The 115-tonne submarines have a crew of only seven. They carry two tiny "chariots" and inflatable boats for transporting the divers. Each *Piranha* may be armed with mines or torpedoes.

Rescue, or combat?

The USSR's *India* submarines are rescue vessels (see page 22). But the two midget craft carried by each one could also be used in combat.

Engines

Two operators

Batteries

Mine being released

Two-seater chariot

Divers can leave a *Piranha* type of submarine and ride on its chariots to an enemy vessel, where they attach magnetic "limpet" mines to the hull. The chariot has no protection so it must be as quiet as possible. It is driven by an almost silent electric motor.

India mother-craft

Tracked submersible leaves

Seabed crawler

Tiny "tracked submersibles" can crawl across the seabed on caterpillar tracks. In combat, they can be used to damage seabed sensors, enter secret naval bases and even lay mines.

SOSUS (SOund SUrveillance System), an unmanned undersea "listening post"

THE YOUNG ENGINEER

The world of attack submarines may seem hi-tech and far-off, as these powerful and expensive craft patrol the world's oceans, ready for action which could have devastating effects. Yet submarines rely on many simple engineering principles. Designers and engineers are continually coming up with new and improved solutions to the problems of moving, steering and navigating under water. Try the projects shown here, which demonstrate some of the basic scientific principles in designing, building and controlling a submarine.

The teardrop shape

Water is difficult to push through, so streamlining is all important (see page 10). Drop a coin into water and it tumbles as it falls. Next, release a teardrop shape of modelling clay tail-first. It falls erratically and may twist round. Release it broad end first. It falls quickly and smoothly.

1 Coin

2 Teardrop (upside down)

3 Teardrop

Going down, coming up

Make a "sub" from a plastic washing-up liquid bottle with a sealed end. Carefully cut two holes in the side and a small hole opposite. Fix a straw into the small hole with modelling clay, making an airtight fit. Seal the end of the straw with tape or clay. Place two lumps of clay near the two lower holes, as "ballast" . Now place your vessel in water. It should float upright (if not, add more ballast). Then take the tape off the end of the straw. This is equivalent to opening the vents to "dive". Air rushes out of the bottle, water rushes in, and the sub dives. Carefully refill it by blowing into the straw, and the sub surfaces (see page 8).

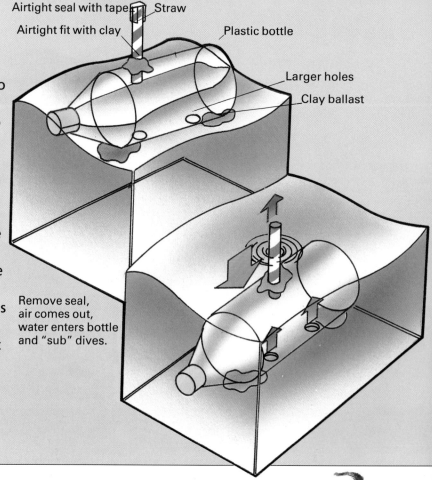

Airtight seal with tape — Straw

Airtight fit with clay

Plastic bottle

Larger holes

Clay ballast

Remove seal, air comes out, water enters bottle and "sub" dives.

The echoes of sonar

Sound travels very well under water. (Many whales, dolphins and other animals can "talk" to each other over great distances.) Imagine that the ripples on the surface of a pool are sound waves. Make a "sound" by dropping in a pebble. Waves spread out, and bounce back off any nearby object. This is like *active sonar*. Rock a toy boat and it makes its own waves. Detecting these is the principle of *passive sonar* (see page 18).

Steering through water

Sets of rudders are used for steering a submarine. Carefully cut three pairs of holes in a plastic bottle and fit straws with card "rudders" attached, as shown below. Add modelling clay ballast so that the vessel stays upright. Push the bottle under and let it fill with water. Then try adjusting the rudders and pushing the "sub" gently with your finger, to make it rise, dive and turn (see page 10).

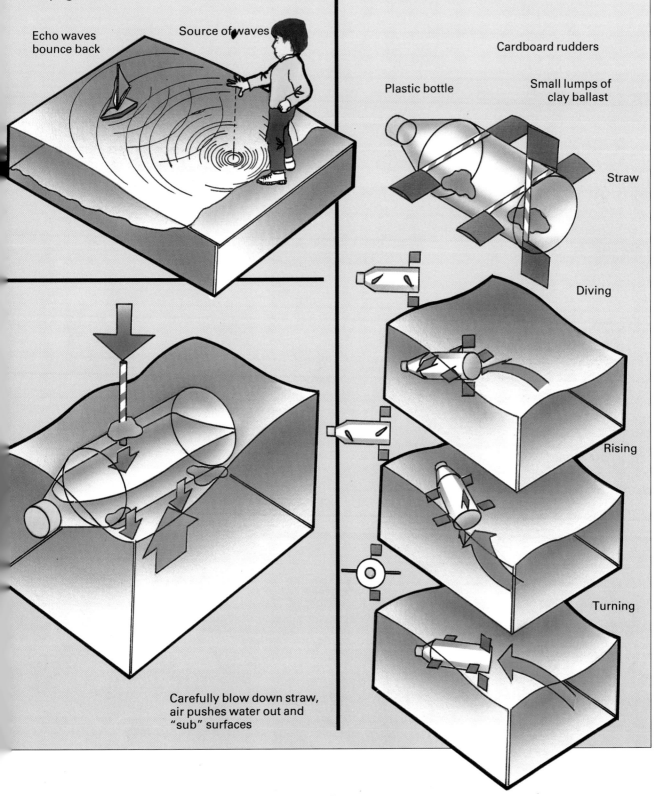

Echo waves bounce back

Source of waves

Cardboard rudders

Plastic bottle

Small lumps of clay ballast

Straw

Diving

Rising

Turning

Carefully blow down straw, air pushes water out and "sub" surfaces

AROUND THE WORLD

Attack submarines are in service with the navies of some 40 countries around the world. They range in size from the Italian *Nazario Sauro* class (SS, 64 metres long) to the Soviet *Sierra* and American *Los Angeles* classes (SSN, 110 metres long). Most are powered by diesel-electric engines. Nearly all submarines have steel hulls, but the Soviet *Alfa* class has a hull made from a metal called titanium. Its advantages are that it is both lighter and stronger than steel. However, titanium is also much more difficult to make and weld than steel. The *Alfa's* light construction, combined with a powerful nuclear engine, gives it a record-breaking top speed of 45 knots (83 kph). Some of the Soviet attack submarines have hydroplanes that can be withdrawn into the hull, to

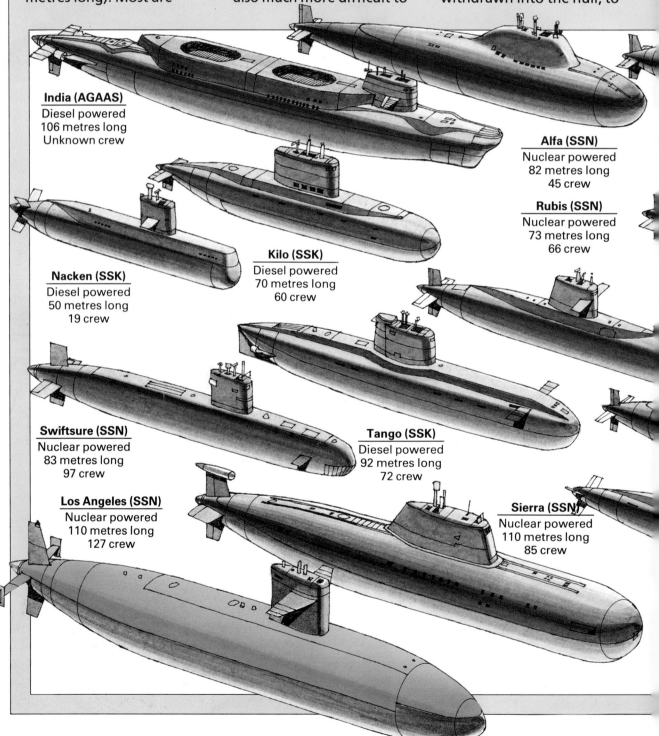

India (AGAAS)
Diesel powered
106 metres long
Unknown crew

Alfa (SSN)
Nuclear powered
82 metres long
45 crew

Rubis (SSN)
Nuclear powered
73 metres long
66 crew

Kilo (SSK)
Diesel powered
70 metres long
60 crew

Nacken (SSK)
Diesel powered
50 metres long
19 crew

Swiftsure (SSN)
Nuclear powered
83 metres long
97 crew

Tango (SSK)
Diesel powered
92 metres long
72 crew

Los Angeles (SSN)
Nuclear powered
110 metres long
127 crew

Sierra (SSN)
Nuclear powered
110 metres long
85 crew

prevent damage from sea ice. The French *Rubis* class are the smallest nuclear-powered submarines built to date. Here are some of the main classes of attack submarines, and their cousins, from navies around the world.

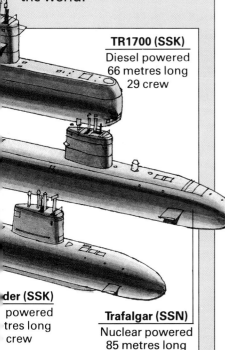

TR1700 (SSK)
Diesel powered
66 metres long
29 crew

...der (SSK)
...powered
...tres long
...crew

Trafalgar (SSN)
Nuclear powered
85 metres long
98 crew

Yushio (SSK)
Diesel powered
76 metres long
80 crew

Zeeleuw (SSK)
Diesel powered
68 metres long
50 crew

Nazario Sauro (SSK)
Diesel powered
64 metres long
49 crew

ASW Anti-Submarine Warfare.

Ballast tanks Tanks which are flooded with water to make a submarine dive.

Complement A submarine's crew.

Depth charge An explosive weapon dropped into the sea near a submarine, set off by water pressure.

DSRV Deep Submergence Rescue Vehicle, a rescue submarine.

ECM Electronic Counter Measures. Using electronic signals to block or confuse ("jam") enemy sensors.

ELF Extremely Low Frequency. A radio communications technique.

Fin The vertical tower on top of a submarine, also called the sail.

Hydrophone An underwater microphone for detecting water-borne sounds.

Hydroplane A control surface or "rudder" used to adjust a submarine's depth.

MAD Magnetic Anomaly Detector, which senses the way that subs and other big, metallic objects bend the Earth's magnetic field.

Periscope A sliding tube giving a view of the surface while the submarine is submerged, housed in the fin.

Radar RAdio Direction And Ranging. A system for finding distant objects by bouncing radio waves off them.

Sonar SOund Navigation And Ranging. A submarine's main sensor system.

SS A diesel-electric submarine.

SSBN A nuclear-powered ballistic missile submarine.

SSG A diesel-electric cruise missile submarine.

SSGN A nuclear-powered cruise missile submarine.

SSK A diesel-electric patrol submarine.

SSN A nuclear-powered attack submarine.

Submersible A small craft that can stay underwater for short periods, normally used with a mother-craft.

Trim The stability of a submarine under water.

VLF Very Low Frequency. A radio communications technique.

INDEX

aerials 16, 17
aluminium 9
ASW 31

ballast 8, 9, 28
ballast tanks 31
batteries 8, 12, 13
Bushnell, David 4

chariots 26, 27
communications 16-7
complement see crew
control room 5, 6, 19
crew 6, 13, 14, 17, 22, 24, 31

depth charge 31
diesel 4, 12, 13, 16, 26
diesel-electric engine 12, 26,
    27, 30
dive 4, 8, 9, 28
Drebbel, Cornelius 4
DSRV 22, 31

ECM 31
ELF 17, 31

fin 4, 5, 16, 31
fuel 12, 26

galley 22
gyroscopes 15

helm 11
HF 14, 16
hull 4, 6, 8-9, 10, 14, 30
hydrophone 18, 20, 21, 31
hydroplane 5, 10, 11, 13, 30,
    31

ice cap 14
image intensifier 19
inertia 15

laser range-finder 19
launch 24-5

MAD 31
mess 22
midget submarines 5, 26, 27
mine 20-1, 27
missile 5, 20-1
module 6
mother-craft 26, 27

Nautilus 12
navigation 14-5
nuclear engine 30
nuclear power 4, 5, 12-3
nuclear reactor 4, 5, 6, 12,
    13, 24, 25
nuclear submarine 18

oxygen 12, 26

periscope 5, 10, 16, 19, 26,
    31
propeller 4, 6, 7, 12
pump-jet 7, 12

radar 5, 16, 31
radio 5, 15, 16, 17
refit 24
rudders 4, 10, 11, 29

seabed 14
SINS 15
slipway 24

sonar 6, 7, 9, 14, 18-9, 22, 26,
    29, 31
SOSUS 27
Soviet 8, 9
SS 4
SSBN 4, 31
SSG 31
SSGN 31
SSK 30, 31
SSN 4, 5, 30, 31
steel 9, 30
streamlining 8, 28
submarine classes 30
submersible 27, 31

TACAMO 17
tactical display screen 19
thermal imager 19
titanium 9, 30
torpedo 5, 20-1, 27
trials 24-5
trim 8, 11, 31
turbines 4, 7, 12, 13
turbulence 6

Photographic Credits:
Cover and page 25: Vickers; pages 9, 10, 11,
15, 16: Salamander Books; pages 12 and 19:
IDR; pages 20, 23 (both), 24:
MoD/Salamander Books; pages 22, 26:
USN/Salamander Books.